BECAUSE
YOU

DO
NOT
ASK

BECAUSE YOU DO NOT ASK

The Hidden Costs of
Not Knowing

Conrod Kelly & Crystal Deazle

Books may be purchased in bulk quantity and/or special sales by
contacting the publisher.

Published by Mynd Matters Publishing
www.myndmatterspublishing.com

978-1-957092-82-9 (pbk)
978-1-957092-83-6 (hdcv)
978-1-957092-84-3 (ebk)

FIRST EDITION

Contents

Maya Roy

D iversity, equity, and inclusion (DEI) can be explored from multiple perspectives: as a leadership practice, a set of tools, and to attract talent for innovation. In this accessible resource, Conrod Kelly and Crystal Deazle demonstrate the value of DEI by working together to offer a practical solution to a systemic issue that frequently loses steam before producing meaningful and sustainable change. With refreshing honesty, they challenge readers to reflect on two important questions. What is the root cause for the lack of ownership for DEI within organizations?? How can we identify, validate, and nurture commitment to DEI as part of assessing, developing, and advancing talent?

With trademark simplicity, Kelly and Deazle have created an invaluable guide for busy hiring managers juggling competing priorities while also passing along their expertise to individuals seeking values-based workplaces. For organizations to not only face but also overcome the geo-political, economic, social, technological, and environmental forces of change, they will need to compete for talent. Diverse talent that exhibits a set of leadership behaviors powered by core values.

Make no mistake, *Because You Do Not Ask* is no superficial checklist for performative DEI. Kelly and Deazle have taken a systems-based approach to building a healthy, sustainable, and agile organizational culture by asking clear, values-based questions.

As technology and artificial intelligence accelerate the pace of change, organizations will need to prioritize self-reflective and critical thinkers who can deconstruct complex problems at all levels of the organization. No issue has been more complex globally than diversity, equity, and inclusion. This concise resource is a guide for self-reflection, external assessments, and robust conversations about DEI as values and core competencies.

My only regret in reading this book is that I did not have this guide when I first started out in my career. Not only would it have saved much heartache, but it would also have been an invaluable resource.

At the end of the day, each one of us is on a unique

leadership journey to find our space in the world. And if we don't ask the right questions of ourselves or surround ourselves with people willing to ask us the tough questions, we risk losing a piece of that journey. As you travel along your path, I hope this guide inspires you to fulfill your purpose and responsibility as a leader.

Conrod Kelly

In 2020, overcome with emotions from the social unrest in the United States sparked by the senseless killings of Black Americans, I woke up early one morning, picked up my phone, and wrote a post on LinkedIn about an epiphany I had around the lack of diversity, equity, and inclusion in US organizations. There were countless debates happening online around where to place the blame, and corporations making financial pledges to solve or silence the issue, but none of it felt like it would address the issues faced by minorities in the workplace and society in a sustainable way.

My post received 121 reactions, 19 comments (about half were my responses to other's comments), and about five reposts. While I didn't expect it to go viral, I did expect more engagement given the conversations that were happening among families, friends, classmates, colleagues, and in all public forums. Maybe I completely misjudged the moment.

Well, why don't I let you read the post for yourself?

"Despite decades of research and initiatives on D&I, very little progress has been made because we are not asking THE right questions or asking THE questions at all. Reflecting on my own experience, at no point during my career have I ever been asked a question about DEI during an interview process as an individual contributor or people leader.

NEVER. Am I the only one?

This means someone can lead a team or organization having never been asked to provide evidence of creating a diverse and inclusive culture, ensuring equity in the hiring and talent management process, or increasing their cultural competence. If that is true, then why would we expect them to hold themselves, their leaders, and their teams accountable?

Diverse & inclusive teams/cultures drive innovation and better results. FACT. So, why doesn't cultural competency weigh heavily in a hiring decision? Think about the message it would send to a current or prospective employee on the value of D&I at the company.

Now imagine this happening in education, healthcare, and government as well.

Ask the right questions, but don't punish people for not getting it right, INITIALLY. Give them the tools to develop the competence and hold them accountable, because product innovation, business results, and the company reputation is at stake."

Initially, the post felt like a raisin in the sun. After a few days, the likes and comments trickled in, and I felt better about not being completely alone in my perspective. I continued tweaking the post to see if it would make a difference, but I finally accepted that the moment was over and a new post would pop into my network's feeds.

About three days later, in between meetings, I casually checked my LinkedIn inbox. Whoa! I couldn't believe it. My post wasn't a dream deferred…it was a dream on a time delay that did explode, releasing a tremendous about of energy and pressure at supersonic speed. *(Read Harlem by Langston Hughes)*

So many people messaged me saying how much they appreciated my post and that they had often wondered the same thing. They reflected on their own experience and realized that not once in their entire career had they been asked a single question about DEI. These are people holding senior positions at Fortune 500 companies. Through our conversations, we arrived at the conclusion that the absence of these questions throughout our careers explained so much about the current state of our organizations. We couldn't say for sure if it was correlation or causation, but it was worth investigating further.

There were several requests for examples of questions, and embarrassingly, I had none. I had ripped open a wound and had nothing to dress it with. I did what anyone would do when forced to come up with an answer to a question they don't know the answer to—I Googled it. I didn't find anything that captured what I would have wanted to be asked, so I wrote my own and sent them out. For the rest of the day, I couldn't shake the feeling that I just might be on to something.

Later that night, I received an email from someone I sent the questions to letting me know that they asked one of the questions in an interview and it completely changed the dynamic of the interview and the ultimate candidate selected. I arrived at work the next day to more emails from people thanking me for my post and requesting examples of questions. Without fail, I would get a follow-up email from people sharing their experience of how asking the questions changed lead candidates to "we dodged a nightmare" candidates based on some of the responses and other candidates to "this is what we need for our culture."

As time passed, I would think of new questions and readily share the list with anyone interested. In the armamentarium of DEI tools, I realized interview questions could be a simple but effective way of producing systemic change in organizations in any industry. With active sponsorship and clear communication from senior leadership and HR, people managers could be held accountable for incorporating DEI questions in the hiring process and when considering performance ratings, promotions, talent designations, and succession planning.

Fast forward two years and I am attending the World Economic Forum Young Global Leaders' Summit in Geneva, Switzerland. I'm truly honored and fortunate to be part of this organization of responsible leaders who are committed to changing the world. A group of us were in a break-out session focused on diversity, equity, and inclusion, and let's just say it wasn't going as expected. I raised my hand and offered an alternative approach to the session. Next thing I know, we are all gathered around a flip chart, most people sitting on the floor, and I'm facilitating the session. After about ninety minutes of deliberation, one of the outcomes from the session was that I needed to write a book on the benefit and hidden cost of not asking DEI questions. So, Maya, Luana, Sinead, and Koaml, this book is because you asked *(more like told)* me to do it!

As you may have noticed on the cover, there are two authors of this book. As I was going through the writing process, I thought it would be great to capture reflections from those in my network whose perspective I valued in the space of DEI. One of the first people I contacted was Crystal Deazle. Over the years we've had conversations, mostly over an amazing meal and game of spades, covering a broad spectrum of topics. However, our most memorable debates dealt with human resources, organizational culture, and DEI. I had always heard the saying that you should never argue with an attorney, but boy do I love a good intellectual tussle. Over nearly two decades of sparring, she's still undefeated.

When she responded to my request to contribute to a specific section of the book, I was so blown away by the perspective she offered that I knew what needed to be done. I asked her to come on board and co-author the book with me, and I politely told her I would not take no for an answer. If you can't beat 'em, join 'em. She kept me waiting for a few days before agreeing to come aboard. I firmly believe this book is fundamentally better because of the intersection of her experience as a lawyer and DEI practitioner and my experience as a business leader and DEI champion.

Crystal Deazle

I was excited when Conrod asked me to contribute an industry insight he could include in his upcoming book. I never imagined that request would lead to an invitation to co-author this book. After much coaxing, I agreed to join forces because his approach to creating diverse, equitable, and inclusive workplaces was novel and simple but revolutionary. If organizations genuinely care about DEI, they must go beyond mere lip service and actively incorporate DEI principles into every stage of the recruiting and leadership management process. By asking critical questions about diversity and inclusion to candidates and leaders alike, companies can foster a culture that embraces the uniqueness and strengths of every individual, ultimately leading to a more vibrant and successful organization.

My DEI journey started many years ago, right after I graduated from law school. I began working as a litigation associate in a big law firm, and it didn't take long to realize that the industry was sorely lacking in diversity, equity, and inclusion. Over the next two decades, I navigated various legal landscapes, working in law firms and law schools. While there were some small steps forward, the truth remained unchanged: the legal industry still fell far short of representing the diverse communities it served.

As a lawyer, I witnessed firsthand the inequalities and lack of diversity within the legal industry, igniting a passion to bring about positive changes. I knew diversity, equity, and inclusion were not just buzzwords but crucial values that needed to be integrated into every aspect of society, including the workplace. My journey into DEI led me to take on roles within organizations where I could influence policies, foster inclusivity, and advocate for marginalized voices.

Through years of practice and learning, I began to see the transformative power of DEI in shaping healthier and more productive work environments. As Conrod and I engaged in our intellectual debates and discussions, it became evident that our combined expertise could create a unique and potent resource for those seeking to build diverse and inclusive organizations. Co-authoring this book allowed me to share my experiences, insights, and strategies for effecting meaningful change in the realm of DEI, and I hope it inspires others to embark on their own journeys toward a more equitable and inclusive workplace and world.

As we neared the completion of writing this content, the Supreme Court's decisions in Students for Fair Admissions v. Harvard University and Students for Fair Admissions v. the University of North Carolina at Chapel Hill dramatically altered fifty years of equal protection laws by eliminating the use of affirmative action in college admissions. While these decisions do not directly pertain to employment, the Court's language seems to encourage heightened scrutiny of corporate diversity efforts, potentially leading to an increase in reverse discrimination employment claims. Consequently, in the face of these changes, it is now more crucial than ever for diversity champions to remain resolute in finding ways to uphold their commitment to DEI.

INTRODUCTION

May your choices reflect your hopes,
not your fears. —Nelson Mandela

Asking DEI questions in the talent acquisition and management process can benefit organizations in several ways. One of the most compelling arguments for doing so is that it can help create a more diverse, equitable, and inclusive workplace. By asking questions about DEI, employers signal to candidates that these **values** are important to the organization. This approach can help attract a diverse pool of candidates, including those who have historically been underrepresented in the industry or organization.

Moreover, integrating DEI questions into talent acquisition and management processes goes beyond merely signaling values. It also demonstrates a commitment to fostering a culture of diversity and inclusion. When candidates witness a company's dedication to these principles, they are more likely to feel welcomed and valued, which can significantly impact their decision to join the organization. Furthermore, the inclusion of DEI considerations throughout the hiring and management journey encourages a greater sense of belonging among employees. As individuals from diverse backgrounds find representation within the organization, it not only fosters a positive work environment but also promotes creativity and innovation. Employees are more likely to bring their unique perspectives, experiences, and skills to the table, leading to fresh ideas and problem-solving approaches. Embracing DEI in the talent process can compel an organization toward greater success and societal impact.

Using DEI questions for leadership placement, especially in internal postings, is particularly important. Doing so can yield valuable insights by uncovering biases and blind spots within the organization or even hidden strengths. This approach not only identifies individuals who can positively impact the culture and overall business, but also ensures leaders align their actions with the values of the organization. For example, asking candidates to provide examples of working with, leading, or building diverse teams. It's also important to solicit feedback from employees who have worked under these leaders, as it provides an opportunity for those who may have been silenced or supported to speak up.

We've both seen and experienced leaders who speak candidly about supporting DEI but have consistently built teams and organizations that are woefully unrepresentative of the available talent pool or the target consumers of their products. At the same time, we've witnessed leaders who not only build diverse teams but excel at soliciting and incorporating different perspectives to enable more effective collaboration and problem-solving within the organization. Having representation is not enough unless there is also inclusion.

> *"Diversity without representation = Inaction*
> *Representation without inclusion = Alienation*
> *Inclusion without equity = Exploitation"*
> —Arthur Chan

In writing, *Because You Do Not Ask*, we wanted to confidently state that these questions can lead to better hiring decisions. By publicly committing to consistently incorporating this component into the talent acquisition and management processes, documenting, and auditing it, organizations will build confidence in their leadership because employees will know they had to demonstrate increasing levels of competence in DEI to advance within the organizations. This simple, structural, and process-driven change can have an immeasurable impact on building a more diverse, inclusive, and effective workforce.

To ensure we captured perspectives from diverse industries, roles, and identities, we have included insights from leading professionals throughout to enhance the credibility and applicability of the tools in this book. These professionals have provided practical guidance from diverse perspectives, empowering readers to take meaningful steps toward creating more diverse, equitable, and inclusive environments.

PART I

CHAPTER I

Making the Case for Change in Your Organization

It's not what you preach, it's what you tolerate
—Jocko Willing

Before diving in, it is important to discuss the terminology we will use throughout the book. The acronym DEI stands for diversity, equity, and inclusion and is used to represent a set of principles and practices aimed at promoting and fostering these aspects within organizations and society at large. JEDI, in the context of DEI, is an expanded acronym that represents a more comprehensive approach to promoting diversity, equity, and inclusion by infusing justice into the analysis.

Diversity refers to the representation and inclusion of individuals from various backgrounds, experiences, and identities, such as race, ethnicity, gender, sexual orientation, age, religion, disability, socioeconomic status, and more. Embracing diversity means acknowledging and valuing the differences that individuals bring to the table and creating an inclusive environment that respects and celebrates this diversity.

Equity involves ensuring fair treatment, opportunities, and access to resources for all individuals, regardless of their backgrounds or characteristics. It acknowledges that people have different starting points and face varying barriers to success. Equity seeks to level the playing field and address systemic disadvantages to create equal opportunities for everyone.

Inclusion focuses on creating a welcoming and supportive environment where all individuals feel valued, respected, and included. It involves fostering a culture that encourages participation, collaboration, and the free expression of diverse perspectives. Inclusive practices ensure that everyone's voices are heard and considered in decision-making processes.

Justice in the DEI framework emphasizes the importance of addressing systemic inequalities and promoting social justice. It involves examining and dismantling the structural barriers that hinder marginalized individuals and groups from accessing equal opportunities and resources.

While our focus is primarily centered on DEI, it is worth noting that the JEDI framework acknowledges that creating a truly inclusive and equitable society requires challenging and transforming systems and institutions that perpetuate discrimination and disadvantage certain groups. The JEDI framework is gaining traction in organizations as it encourages a more holistic approach to building a more just and inclusive world.

We wrote this book with inclusivity in mind, catering to job seekers, hiring managers, HR professionals, DEI practitioners, and DEI champions. Throughout your career journey, you may oscillate between these positions or even occupy multiple roles simultaneously. Therefore, the "you" we reference in the title is, in fact, you—the valued reader!

Our aim is to encourage and empower you to embrace the power of questions in transforming your organization's and your own commitment to DEI. Over the course of several chapters, we will advocate for integrating DEI questions into all stages of the talent-management process. By asking these critical questions, you send a powerful signal that the historical status quo is no longer acceptable. Systemic barriers to advancing DEI within an organization have been perpetuated by allowing individuals with explicit and implicit biases to reach senior levels, leading to structural bias that negatively impacts company culture and hiring practices. Infusing DEI questions signals your organization's commitment to creating a more inclusive and equitable workplace and reduces the likelihood of having these biases impair an organization from the beginning.

Effectively making the case for change requires two essential elements: personal stories and data. As a mentor once advised, never tell a story without data, and never present data without a story. Stories serve as the messengers of culture, providing insights into the past and present while communicating the desired culture for the future. Similarly, data serves the same purpose, as you can use it to quantify the extent of the problem found in the stories, articulate the ambition or desired state, and communicate the pace of progress.

The best place to start is with your own stories and data. For example:

- How often have you researched a company's commitment to DEI? Why were you interested in this information? How did what you learned influence your decision? If you haven't, why didn't you think to investigate?

- How have you communicated your commitment to DEI in your resume or leadership narrative?

What data did you use to substantiate your commitment? Why did you choose to communicate this? If you haven't, how would you explain the absence?

- In what percentage of interviews have you asked questions specific to DEI as a hiring manager? Why were you asking? What did you learn? If you haven't, why do you think it didn't happen? What could you have learned?

- How often have you asked questions specific to DEI as a candidate? Why were you asking? What did you learn? If you haven't, why do you think it didn't happen? What could you have learned?

By combining personal stories and data, organizations can compellingly advocate for change. These two essential elements work hand in hand, reinforcing each other's impact. Personal stories bring the human aspect to the forefront, allowing stakeholders to connect emotionally with individuals' experiences and understand the present challenges. These stories also provide a glimpse into the desired culture for the future, shaping the narrative of the organization's transformation journey.

On the other hand, data provides the necessary empirical evidence to back up these stories, quantifying the magnitude of the issues highlighted and illustrating the urgency for change. It enables leaders to articulate clear goals and ambitions, chart the path toward the desired state, and track the progress made along the way. By seamlessly weaving personal stories and data together, organizations can foster a deeper understanding of the need for change and mobilize support from stakeholders at all levels.

Industry Insight

Lili Gil Valleta, CEO and Co-Founder, Culture+ Group

Given today's rapidly shifting demographics and how these dynamics are reshaping people's and stakeholder expectations, it is critical for any leader to understand and clearly articulate the why behind the what of DEI. That is why to successfully lead any team or organization into their next chapter for growth and competitiveness, people leaders must be able to clearly demonstrate their Cultural Intelligence® coefficient. That is embodied by a mindset and stories that show they are aware, understand and apply cultural competence and inclusive data into their everyday business and people decisions. This capability transcends simply acknowledging that "diversity is important," but it comes with the demonstrated understanding of the case for action (in numbers) for how leading and advancing DEI ties directly into the team's ability to innovate, achieve their full potential, and outperform the competition.

While the business case for increased diversity, equity, and inclusion in organizations may be obvious or well-known and understood by some, the pace of progress suggests there is more work to do. As more and more companies have begun to lean into DEI, especially post-George Floyd, there has been an explosion of data and stories from globally respected consultancies, academic institutions, and publications. The value of these institutions increasing their research has been the ability to go beyond the moral argument for DEI*, which remains the strongest rationale, but also to explore the business case for diversity.

Sidebar on the moral case for DEI. Two of the best business models in the world are also the most immoral—slavery and child labor. There was no compelling "business case" to end chattel slavery. Thankfully, a moral argument was made to legally eradicate it, although one could argue that it has been replaced by modern-day slavery. The same can be said for child labor, which still affects 1 in 7 children globally and is used to produce many of the goods consumed in Western markets.

The ten points below can serve as a foundation for adopting DEI questions and contribute to creating a more diverse, equitable, and inclusive organization. By combining personal stories and empirical data, these points can be reinforced and articulated with real-life experiences and evidence.

1. **Diverse teams are more innovative:** Diverse teams bring different perspectives, experiences, and ideas to the table, resulting in more innovative solutions and products. Companies with diverse teams are more likely to develop new products and services that meet the needs of a broader range of customers. **Companies with above-average diversity scores generate 19% more revenue from innovation than those with below-average diversity scores.** (Boston Consulting Group)

2. **Increased revenue and profits:** Studies have shown that companies with diverse teams are

more profitable and have higher revenue. **Gender-diverse companies are 15% more likely to outperform their peers, while ethnically diverse companies are 35% more likely to outperform their peers.** (McKinsey & Company)

3. **Higher employee engagement and retention:** Employees are more engaged and committed to their work when they feel valued and included. This leads to higher retention rates, reducing turnover costs. **Companies with diverse teams have a 22% lower turnover rate than companies without diverse teams.** (Forbes)

4. **Improved decision-making:** Diverse teams make better decisions as they consider multiple viewpoints, reducing the risk of groupthink. Diverse teams can collaborate more effectively, leveraging different strengths and experiences to achieve shared goals. **Gender-diverse teams make better decisions than all-male teams 73% of the time.** (Harvard Business Review)

5. **Enhanced brand reputation:** Companies with diverse teams are perceived as more socially

responsible, attracting employees, customers, and investors who value diversity. **71% of millennials say they would prefer to work for a company with a strong commitment to diversity and inclusion.** (Deloitte)

6. **Increased creativity:** Diverse teams can generate more creative ideas by bringing together a variety of perspectives and experiences. **Diverse teams outperform non-diverse teams by 50% when it comes to generating creative ideas.** (Harvard Business Review)

7. **Enhanced problem-solving:** Diverse teams can solve complex problems more effectively, drawing from a broader range of knowledge and skills. Diverse teams can adapt more quickly to changing circumstances, leading to better organizational agility. **Diverse teams can solve problems faster than homogeneous teams, taking 60% less time to decide.** (Harvard Business Review)

8. **Better talent acquisition:** A commitment to diversity, equity, and inclusion can help attract

top talent from a wider range of backgrounds. **67% of job seekers consider workplace diversity an important factor when considering job offers.** (Glassdoor)

9. **Improved customer satisfaction:** Diverse teams can provide valuable insights into the needs and preferences of diverse customer groups. Being able to better understand and serve the needs of diverse customer bases can lead to higher customer satisfaction and loyalty. Companies with diverse teams are also better positioned to compete in diverse markets. **Companies with above-average diversity scores have a 45% larger market share than those with below-average diversity scores.** (Boston Consulting Group)

10. **Reduced legal risks:** Prioritizing DEI can lead to a more inclusive workplace, mitigating discrimination and lowering the likelihood of facing lawsuits. A study by the Center for American Progress revealed that that companies with more diverse workforces were less likely to face discrimination lawsuits. **Specifically, companies with the highest**

levels of racial and ethnic diversity had a 35% lower chance facing lawsuits when compared to those with the lowest levels of diversity.

Industry Insight

Texanna Reeves, Vice President DEI & Associate Experience, Rite Aid Corporation

It is essential to leverage data to advance your DEI initiatives because data can tell a compelling story that has a greater impact. Note these tips:

- *Align metrics to business strategic initiatives. Example: Increase in diverse hires for positions essential to the company.*

- *Use metrics executive leadership recognizes. Partner with Finance to agree on metrics and their calculations. Example: the cost of turnover can be a big number, but if Finance thinks the number is inflated, this measurement will be dismissed.*

- *Maintain data integrity. Audit your data for completeness, accuracy, and reliability to create trust. Lack of trust in the numbers can negatively impact professional credibility.*

- ***Identify conclusions.** When you show graphs or charts, always display key findings in clear language to avoid guesswork.*

- ***Tell a story.** Stories bring data to life. One way to develop your narrative is to include quotes or experiences from your employees.*

Adapted Excerpt from RESTAGED:
A Mental Model for Personal and Professional
Growth by Conrod Kelly

The work of advancing DEI can be emotionally and physically draining. At times, you may be tempted to leave and find another organization (using some of the tips in this book) that is more advanced in its DEI journey. That decision is a personal one and should be thoroughly interrogated. When I have encountered this dilemma in my career, I would stop to ask myself, "Am I growing where I'm planted?"

Throughout your career, it is not uncommon to question if you're at the right place. These feelings often spring up when a job doesn't feel as satisfying as expected, usually because of the leader you are working for. Often, the initial thinking is to uproot and start over somewhere else or venture out on your own. I'll be the first to say I have left an organization, stayed at an organization, and even started my own, all out of frustration with the lack of progress on DEI. All these decisions had a positive impact on my career because the decision to stay, leave, or venture out was made based on asking myself if I was growing in my environment.

There are two questions I always ask in making the decision. The first is, can I dig deeper? Often, our first reaction to the status quo on DEI is an emotional reaction. I have no issue with that because it's a natural, human response to a trigger. Once I'm able to process the emotion, I transition to using logic to better understand the who, what, when, where, and why. This isn't done in isolation. I connect with people in my network to listen to their experiences and bounce ideas off each other until we can get to a root cause. This led me to the epiphany that prompted the writing of this book. Another tangible example is OneTen®, which identified a four-year degree as a barrier to well-paying career opportunities for Black talent leading to a pivot across many organizations to skills-based hiring.

The second question is, have I planted seeds? Sometimes, the lack of change stems from not planting enough seeds. I have spoken with far too many people who were frustrated with the conditions at their company, but never spoke up about them or proposed plausible solutions. Planting seeds is about leading the way by being the change you wish to see. The feeling of being stuck is often caused by deference, a weed that can limit growth. Sometimes, we must remove our own self-defeating beliefs (pull the weeds) to open ourselves and our organizations to new opportunities.

When all else fails, transplanting can be a great option. Seeds are often started in one location and then replanted somewhere else. Some of us may have been in locations for too long and the time has come to move so we can continue to grow. Nevertheless, the work you do before leaving will help you grow where you are planted next. Advancing DEI requires agility, resilience, and a healthy relationship with risk.

Organizations and leaders take risks every day. The risks they take can contribute to the growth of the organization just as the risks they are unwilling to take can cost the organization. The better you are at using stories and data to talk about risk, the better you will be at making the case for change in your organization.

Never make a permanent decision on a temporary situation —T.D. Jakes

CHAPTER II

DEI: The Leadership Catalyst

> *"If your actions inspire others to dream more, learn more, do more and become more, you are a leader."*
> —President John Quincy Adams

The term "leadership catalyst" refers to a person who sparks or accelerates significant positive change or growth within an organization or a group of individuals. A leadership catalyst acts as a trigger or catalyst for transformation, often bringing about a shift in mindset, behavior, or approach among leaders, which translates to improved performance, innovation, and positive outcomes. This concept implies that certain individuals have the power to stimulate positive change and propel organizations forward.

In today's fast-changing global landscape, the significance of traditional leadership abilities has diminished, albeit not completely. The focus is now on the indispensable soft skills required to drive performance within large, complex, and data-driven organizations. Leaders within these organizations must invest substantial time in collaborating across functions to foster understanding, consensus, and alignment. Beyond allocating financial and human resources to exploit opportunities, rectify issues, and mitigate risks, leaders must also cultivate an extensive external network of critical relationships encompassing diverse constituencies. The soft skills embedded in diversity, equity, and inclusion lie at the intersection of mastering the internal and external environment. Soft skills encompass many personal attributes, including communication abilities and social competencies that enable individuals to interact effectively with others. They include skills such as written and verbal communication, empathy, adaptability, collaboration, and emotional intelligence (EQ). According to one LinkedIn survey, 92% of hiring managers in the United States believe that soft skills are equally or more important than hard skills when it comes to transformative leadership.

With the proliferation of artificial intelligence and automation taking over tasks that require technical skills (hard skills) in organizations, the ability to outperform competitors will rely heavily on the power of leaders to unlock the potential of individuals, teams, and networks through inclusive leadership, a core DEI component. Creating an inclusive environment cultivates opportunities to build relationships with people from various backgrounds. Research by McPherson, Smith-Lovin, and Cook in 2001 shows that having diverse social networks broaden individuals' access to information, resources, and perspectives, enabling them to have vast networks, build stronger relationships, and be more adept at influencing others to drive change.

Inclusive leadership provides a unique advantage. When leaders cultivate an inclusive environment, they open doors for collaboration with individuals from diverse backgrounds. This fosters a broader range of perspectives and ideas while improving access to valuable information and resources. As a result, leaders with diverse networks can build strong relationships with a wide range of stakeholders, making them more effective at driving positive change within their organizations and in the larger community. Inclusive leadership is a powerful tool for staying ahead of the competition and achieving long-term success in an ever-changing world.

The importance of DEI acumen has been heightened due to the elevated expectations placed upon leaders to be visible and engaging, internally and externally. Leaders must now be able to engage personally, transparently, and with accountability, with the added complexity of social media platforms where information and opinions can be rapidly disseminated. Leaders must remain acutely attuned to how various audiences perceive their decisions, as minor lapses in achieving intended outcomes with a handful of employees or constituents can have detrimental consequences. Hence, the importance of DEI cannot be overstated.

As companies look to reimagine leadership development, we cannot overemphasize the importance of placing leaders in roles that necessitate interaction with diverse employees and external constituencies. There is still a place for rotating individuals through different departments and countries and placing them in executive development programs. However, exposing leaders to different cultures and perspectives is the best way to foster cultural competence. This is not an opinion but something Conrod has personally experienced living and working in another country where he did not know the language or the culture but ran an organization with more than 14 nationalities. Exposure to diverse cultures also enhances individuals' abilities to navigate complex global environments, establish rapport across cultural boundaries, and effectively lead diverse teams.

In the past, the evaluation of leaders often revolved around their ability to deliver financial results. How they achieved those results were seldom evaluated explicitly, systematically, or objectively. Some companies are making progress in assessing leaders' DEI competence and the diversity of their organizations and incorporating it into performance evaluations and compensation. However, more needs to be done to evaluate DEI proficiency and its impact on leadership aptitude for continued growth.

As the U.S. prepares for a majority-minority society by 2040, global population shifts accelerate due to climate change, and political instability reshapes the demographic in countries across several contents, leaders will face an even greater challenge in addressing issues of diversity and inclusion. Those leaders with advanced DEI abilities will be able to publicly, empathetically, proactively, and effortlessly navigate various employee groups, ensuring their voices are heard, representing their interests, and fostering an environment where diverse talent thrives.

We wrote this book because very few organizations invest in training to improve the interviewing skills of those involved in the talent process, especially for leadership roles where candidates are presumed to possess the requisite background and perspective to lead a diverse organization. We believe companies must develop new tools, or leverage the ones provided throughout these pages, to establish an objective basis for evaluating and comparing DEI competency, thereby removing affinity bias from the hiring process. While some organizations use personality and behavioral tests in the hiring process, there is limited use of tests to evaluate DEI competency.

Ultimately, companies must not only develop and evaluate the DEI competency of individual leaders but also entire leadership teams. Weakness or ineptitude on the part of any team member can have a systemic effect on the group. A study conducted by Catalyst, a global nonprofit organization, discovered that employees who perceive their organization as fair and equitable are more likely to exhibit higher levels of empathy, communication, and collaboration. Where employees perceive fairness and equity is in their direct manager, hence why it is so important to have leaders that excel at DEI.

Will asking DEI questions help companies make more informed decision? The answer hinges, in part, on their ability to effectively evaluate the DEI competency of candidates and whether they choose to make DEI competency an integral component of their talent management strategies. It is our hope that this book challenges undergraduate, graduate, and executive education programs to place an emphasis on DEI. We also see an opportunity for organizations to devise innovative mechanisms for identifying and assessing candidates based on their DEI competence.

Our goal is to make it evident that organizations must fundamentally reassess their existing practices to thrive in an increasingly challenging business environment and offer simple and sustainable solutions to effectively remove systemic barriers to diversity, equity, and inclusion. We cannot overemphasize the importance of simple and sustainable solutions as they protect organizations from diversity retreat – the walking back of commitments and budget cuts to DEI initiatives when faced with financial pressures or "competing" priorities.

So far, we have made the business case for DEI and DEI as a leadership catalyst, and now we want to pivot to job seekers to help them identify organizations that have a genuine commitment to DEI. Individuals should look for companies that make public their DEI goals, progress or lack thereof, and sustained actions to promote a truly inclusive workplace. By aligning themselves with organizations that prioritize DEI, job seekers can contribute to and thrive in environments that value and empower individuals from diverse backgrounds.

PART II

CHAPTER III

Researching Whether a Company is Committed to DEI

Vision without action is a dream. Action without vision is a nightmare —Japanese Proverb

An emerging trend when considering whether to join an organization is its commitment to DEI. For job seekers, when an organization is committed to DEI, it creates a more inclusive and welcoming workplace where people from diverse backgrounds can thrive because they feel valued and respected. The proof of this often shows up in greater job satisfaction scores and higher retention rates.

After the tragic murder of George Floyd in 2020, the expectation for companies to support social justice increased in importance for job seekers, especially those from minority communities. The focus on justice drove the transformation of DEI to JEDI, acknowledging the important role companies can play in shaping public policy and sentiment. Company statements on their website and social media platforms are a good start, but the public wants to hear directly from the CEO about concrete, sustainable investments and actions the company is taking to help address discrimination and inequality in the workplace and society.

Nike is a notable example of a company that took a stand for social justice. In 2018, Nike released a powerful ad campaign featuring Colin Kaepernick, a former NFL quarterback known for kneeling during the national anthem to protest racial injustice and police brutality. The campaign's tagline was "Believe in something. Even if it means sacrificing everything." Nike's decision to feature Kaepernick in their ad generated significant controversy, with some people criticizing the company and calling for boycotts. However, the campaign resonated with many consumers who supported Kaepernick's stance and admired Nike's willingness to address social issues.

Despite the backlash, Nike's sales surged following the ad's release. The company reported a 31% increase in online sales in the immediate aftermath, and its stock value reached an all-time high. The campaign helped strengthen Nike's brand image among younger, socially conscious consumers and sparked a broader conversation about activism and corporate responsibility. This example illustrates that taking a stand for social justice can align a company with consumers who share their values, increase brand loyalty, and financial success. However, it's important to note that the impact of such stands can vary depending on various factors, including the specific social issue, the target market, and the company's overall brand positioning.

One of the most telling signs of an organization's commitment to DEI is its ability to attract and retain diverse talent, especially at the highest levels. If the organization's leadership or executive team lacks diversity, which includes having only one person from an underrepresented group in its ranks, it will generate skepticism. Additionally, if there is higher diversity observed in both numbers and representation at lower levels that falls of dramatically as you look higher in the organization, it may lead some to conclude that systemic barriers are hindering the advancement of diverse talent.

In such a scenario, the organization must acknowledge the need for a more robust and inclusive approach to promote diversity and equity at all levels of the organization. This involves not only recruiting diverse talent but also creating an inclusive work environment where diverse perspectives are valued and where all employees have equal opportunities for growth and advancement. By actively fostering a culture that celebrates diversity and promotes a sense of belonging, the organization can demonstrate a genuine commitment to DEI principles.

Moreover, transparency in reporting and sharing progress on diversity goals can help build trust and accountability with stakeholders. Embracing DEI as a strategic imperative not only aligns with social and ethical responsibilities but also serves as a driving force behind innovation, productivity, and overall organizational success.

An often overlooked but essential element of an organization's commitment to DEI is its brand reputation. While consumer product goods companies find it easier to create a positive brand reputation, it is also achievable in any industry through intentional efforts to build strong relationships with communities. A strong brand reputation, particularly with underrepresented groups, indicates that the company has earned consumers' trust by being purposeful, present, and persistent. Companies like Coca-Cola, Procter & Gamble, Cadillac, PepsiCo, Walmart, and McDonald's have successfully established strong ties with diverse communities. However, it's crucial to note that a positive brand reputation is not always synonymous with a strong DEI culture.

For instance, despite Nike's stand in 2018, the company faced criticism and backlash for the lack of diverse representation in its ranks, particularly in executive leadership roles and its internal diversity and inclusion practices. In 2018, a group of female Nike employees conducted a survey to assess the company's workplace culture and found evidence of pay disparities and gender discrimination. This led to a broader discussion about DEI within the company, prompting Nike to publicly acknowledge the need for improvement. Nike has since made efforts to address these concerns. In 2019, the company announced goals to increase the representation of women and historically underrepresented individuals at various levels within its workforce, including senior leadership roles. They also implemented initiatives like employee training programs and mentorship opportunities to foster a more inclusive workplace. However, despite these steps, criticism of Nike's DEI practices has persisted, facing calls for internal reform to ensure diversity and inclusion across all operations. Some advocates argue that the company's senior leadership team still does not reflect its customer base's diversity or adequately addresses marginalized communities' experiences and perspectives.

You may be wondering, if Nike has all these internal issues with diversity, how are they able to connect with diverse communities. Part of the answer lies in their Business Diversity & Inclusion or supplier diversity programs, where it partners with groups from diverse communities to reach the community. This is why a company's commitment to supplier diversity is another area we urge people to investigate. Supplier diversity is an often-overlooked aspect of DEI. Supplier diversity programs aim to increase opportunities for historically disadvantaged groups, such as minority-owned, women-owned, LGBTQIA+-owned, disability-owned, and veteran-owned businesses. By evaluating a company's commitment to supplier diversity, we can determine if they are actively working to create a more inclusive and equitable business model. Supporting diverse suppliers can help stimulate economic growth within underrepresented communities. Diverse suppliers often bring unique perspectives, innovative ideas, and specialized expertise to the table, which can ultimately improve a company's competitiveness in the marketplace. Many of the companies who spend more than $1 billion annually with diverse suppliers are also the companies with the greatest brand loyalty, the most admired, and have consistently strong financial performance. Examples include Apple, Google, IBM, Microsoft, Bank of America, JP Morgan Chase & Co, COMCAST, AT&T, Verizon, Ford, GM, Honda, Toyota, CVSHealth, Kaiser Permanente, Johnson & Johnson, Merck, Procter & Gamble, and Walmart.

Industry Insight

Amy Gómez, Ph.D., SVP, Diversity Strategy, Klick Health

Research on a company's commitment to DEI–both in its public statements and its actions–is a critical part of candidate interview preparation.

If the candidate is diverse (by any dimension of diversity: race, ethnicity, gender, sexual identity, ability, neurodiversity, etc.), the company's commitment will determine the quality of the candidate's employee experience. Will they develop a sense of belonging or be subject to frequent micro-aggressions? Will they be offered substantive opportunities for training and advancement, or will those opportunities be assigned to their non-diverse colleagues? Are there programs dedicated to creating systemic change to ensure future cohorts of leadership reflect the diversity of the markets where the company operates?

The value of this research is not limited to diverse candidates. For committed DEI allies, a company's stated commitments and demonstrated efforts indicate how closely the company's values align with their own. Allyship in action can only thrive within environments where being a vocal advocate is perceived as a positive.

Quick Tips on Researching a Company's Commitment to DEI

- **Company website:** Check if the company has a section dedicated to diversity, equity, and inclusion. If they do, look for information about their initiatives, goals, and progress. You may also be able to find information in their ESG report. While on the company site, look at the leadership team and their bios. Another important source of information are job postings. Beyond what is required to be included by law, are there other signals in the preferred or required experiences that signal DEI is important to the hiring manager and the organization?

- **Social media:** Follow the organization's social media accounts and look for posts and updates related to diversity, equity, and inclusion. These accounts can give you a sense of whether the organization prioritizes these issues and effectively communicates that position with its stakeholders.

- **News articles and press releases:** Search for news articles and press releases about the organization's diversity, equity, and inclusion efforts. This can help you understand its current and past initiatives and any controversies or challenges faced.

- **Employee reviews:** Check out websites like Glassdoor or Indeed to see what current and former employees say about the organization's culture and overall commitment to diversity, equity, and inclusion.

- **Diversity reports and rankings:** Some organizations participate in annual diversity reports and rankings that provide data and insights about their workforce demographics and diversity initiatives. You can search for these reports on their websites or through a search engine.

- **Industry benchmarks:** Look for industry benchmarks and best practices related to diversity, equity, and inclusion. This can help you understand how the organization compares to its peers based on the expectations within a given industry.

Industry Insight

Yael Hernandez-Azeke, Senior Manager, Employee Success – Internal Mobility, Salesforce

When evaluating a company, a few general themes should be addressed:

Pay Equity – *DEI initiatives should support achieving pay equity across an organization. It is important for candidates to understand the company's philosophy, approach, and results regarding pay equity, regardless of their gender identity. There have been numerous examples of companies being found liable for pay inequity with underrepresented minorities and women. Some of the* factors that can contribute to pay inequity is where a company chooses to source talent for certain roles (e.g., select colleges/universities with limited diversity), preferring college degrees over technical experience for certain roles, and in absence of a standard approach to how people can advance in the organization (e.g., overreliance on sponsorship, non-structured interview processes, or assessment tools that may disproportionately eliminate certain groups).

Promotional opportunities – It is not enough to achieve diverse representation at entry-levels. Companies should demonstrate a commitment to maintaining or improving representation at all levels of the organization. Candidates should investigate how the company handles employee development (e.g., internal/external programs for underrepresented groups), if there is equity in the pace of advancement (e.g., one group not advancing at an accelerated pace versus others), and the ability to move within and outside of a specific area in the company (e.g., does a specific department over-index with one group who has difficulty moving within the company).

ESG – One specific area within ESG we recommend investigating is a company's investment in the communities where they operate, and the consumers they *serve. Although these investments provide a glimpse into the company's values, there is still a need to exercise caution. Candidates must research how the work is decided, led, and measured. One of the mistakes people make often is assuming diversity in a company's marketing campaigns or their investments in certain communities reflect the culture of the organization. The employee experience is where DEI matters and has a tangible impact.*

For job seekers that prioritize DEI values, researching a company's commitment to these principles is crucial. Understanding a company's stated commitments and demonstrated efforts can help in assessing the alignment between their own values and the organization's. By conducting thorough research and considering various factors, individuals can make informed decisions about joining organizations that are truly committed to creating inclusive and equitable workplaces.

CHAPTER IV

How to Communicate Your Commitment to DEI

If you are going to hold an organization accountable for its commitment to DEI, you must also be accountable as well. As a job seeker, one way to signal that you value DEI is through your resume. Using this tool to communicate your commitment to DEI can help position you as someone who shares the organization's values.

If you have experience working on DEI initiatives or have skills related to promoting diversity and inclusion, including this information in your resume can help you stand out from other candidates who may not have emphasized this aspect of their experience or values. Even without extensive experience or skills, including information about your commitment to DEI can also demonstrate your willingness to contribute to a company's efforts to create a more diverse and inclusive workplace.

However, it is important to ensure that any information you include in your resume about your commitment to DEI is relevant to the job you are applying for and presented professionally and appropriately. The one thing we would caution anyone against is overstating or falsifying any statements related to DEI. A diverse panel or one with high DEI acumen will be able to discern if the responses reflect theory versus practice, and are authentic.

We must also acknowledge that there is a risk in disclosing your DEI commitment as it creates an opportunity for bias. But if it does, you then can assess whether it is truly a company or leader for which you would want to work. Being honest and transparent about your DEI acumen presents a chance to assess whether the organization truly values DEI principles and whether it aligns with your values and aspirations. Ultimately, applying to an organization prioritizing DEI can lead to a more fulfilling and meaningful career.

Quick Tips for Communicating Your Commitment to DEI in Your Resume

- **Use keywords:** Incorporate relevant keywords such as "diversity," "equity," "inclusion," "cultural competence," "psychological safety," etc., in your resume. This will help your resume stand out to employers who are looking for candidates who prioritize DEI.

- **Highlight DEI-related experiences:** In your education, work, or extracurricular experience sections, highlight any experiences you've had that relate to diversity, equity, and inclusion. For example, you might mention any leadership roles you've held in organizations focused on DEI, any diversity-related training you've received, or any initiatives you've spearheaded to increase diversity and inclusion in your workplace.

- **Showcase your language abilities:** If you are bilingual or multilingual, highlight this in your resume. Being able to communicate in multiple languages is an asset to organizations looking to promote diversity and inclusion.

- **Use a DEI statement:** Consider including a DEI statement in your resume. This is a short statement that communicates your commitment to diversity, equity, and inclusion. Here's an example: "I am committed to creating a workplace that values diversity, equity, and inclusion. I believe that diversity of thought, experience, and background is essential to driving innovation and success, and I am dedicated to fostering an inclusive environment where everyone feels valued and respected."

- **Tailor your resume to the job:** Finally, as with any resume, it should be tailored to the job for which you're applying. If the job description emphasizes the importance of DEI, make sure to highlight your relevant experiences and skills. For example, if the job involves working with diverse populations, emphasize any experiences you've had working with people from different cultures or backgrounds.

Industry Insight

Regine Moore, Director, Constituent Relations, Walmart

As someone who has worked in multicultural media, multicultural marketing, and now a leader in Constituent

Relations, DEI has been central to my roles. While listing my roles may explain what I did, it doesn't capture why I did it. My passion for this work stems from a core desire to match people-centric problem solving with inclusive-collaborations. Culturally connected solutions require, or I dare say, demands a consistent and trusted partner to authentically showcase their story in a way that highlights the struggle, but even more importantly, the beauty and the awe that exists within the fabric of diverse individuals and communities. I live each day in the hope that my work can better the life of just one. With that, I strive to be a servant leader, guided by empathy, who creates strategic partnerships with individuals and organizations to help build a more equitable and just society. Keeping this as the focus will always advance the company's mission and vision.

These characteristics I've highlighted, reflect a good leader. Not a Black leader, or female leader, or a DEI professional. My hope is that people continue to understand that DEI is foundational to leadership, and it will become easier to weave this into the DNA of your team and your company culture.

Adapted Excerpt from RESTAGED

Hands down, one of my favorite songs growing up was, *This Little Light of Mine*. When I got to the part that says, "I'm going to let it shine," I made sure everyone knew how serious I was by trying to sing as loud as the choir. The song taught me at an early age that we all have light within, and we have a responsibility to use it so others may see the positive things we are doing. In the DEI space, one must know the difference between artificial and natural light, because the diverse audiences you may be trying to build a relationship with will quickly and easily discern the difference. If your commitment to DEI is natural, then you don't have to worry about who is around or not wanting to say the wrong thing, because it's not a performance, it's just who you are.

One of the common pitfalls I've witnessed are individuals cutting corners on their DEI learning journey. One book, film, podcast, conference, course, protest, trip to the inner city, yard-sign, t-shirt, vote, conversation, friend, etc. (you get the point) does not make you a DEI expert or ally. Shortcutting your learning will shortchange your impact and future market value. To complete the light metaphor, **do not make the mistake of being all shine and no substance.**

One of the best ways to communicate your commitment to DEI is making it part of your brand. Your personal and professional success is intrinsically linked to your brand. Even if you do not create one for yourself, a brand will be created for you. The second you fail to realize that you are a brand, is the moment you lose competitiveness in the market. The foundation of a brand is trust, just like in a relationship. Your personal brand is directly correlated to your relationships with people. People will trust your brand when their experience consistently meets or beats their expectations.

Developing your personal brand should be an intentional and strategic exercise to demonstrate your value proposition. Now that social media is integrated into our daily lives, there is additional risk and reward by being discoverable by the entire world. Even if you are not against advancing DEI, if you don't appear to be for it through your words, actions, and habits, people can draw conclusions about your commitment. Even one lapse in judgment, especially related to DEI, can require significant time and effort to remedy, or be insurmountable. Therefore, we cannot stress enough how important it is for your leadership narrative to be authentic, compelling, and consistent. Making DEI part of your brand can help enhance your visibility, expand your network, and attract new opportunities. In the process of building your brand, you may also learn things about yourself that can make you more relatable to a broader audience.

CHAPTER V

How to Credibly Address Knowledge or Skills Gaps Related to DEI

Sometimes the wrong choices bring us to the right places. Sometimes you make choices in life and sometimes choices make you. Freedom is realizing you have a choice. —T. F. Hodge

As we shared at the end of Chapter IV, it's important to be honest about your level of experience with diversity, equity, and inclusion while still showing your willingness to learn and improve. You can explain that while you haven't had many opportunities to work with DEI in the past, you are committed to educating yourself and developing the necessary skills to contribute positively to a diverse and inclusive workplace.

Depending on many factors, DEI may be a daily, unavoidable, burdensome topic or something that is never thought of or discussed because your environment doesn't warrant it. In both scenarios and all the scenarios in between, there is still an opportunity to learn.

Quick Tips to Help You Address a Lack of DEI Experience

- **Acknowledge your limitations:** Be honest and upfront about your lack of experience in DEI. This shows that you are self-aware and willing to learn.

- **Share what you know:** Even if you don't have direct experience with DEI, you may have some knowledge or understanding of the topic. Share any relevant information you have, such as books or articles you've read or any training you've received.

- **Highlight your willingness to learn:** Show that you are eager and willing to learn about DEI. Share any steps you have taken to educate yourself on the topic or your plans to continue learning.

- **Connect your skills to DEI:** Think about how your skills and experiences can be applied to DEI. For example, if you have experience working with diverse groups of people or leading teams, talk about how those skills can be applied to a DEI context.

- **Ask questions:** Don't be afraid to ask the interviewer questions about their DEI initiatives or what they are looking for in a candidate. This shows that you are interested and engaged in the topic.

Remember, DEI is a continuous learning process, no one is expected to have all the answers. Depending on the context, the definition of DEI can change, creating an advantage or disadvantage for someone based on their experience. What is most important is that you are genuinely willing to listen, learn, and grow.

By embracing an open mindset and actively seeking opportunities to educate yourself on DEI topics, you can better navigate the complexities of diverse and inclusive organizations. Engaging in workshops, seminars, and reading materials that explore various perspectives will enhance your understanding and ability to engage in meaningful conversations about DEI matters. Additionally, valuing the insights and experiences of others can lead to more inclusive and empathetic interactions within your workplace and beyond. Fostering an inclusive environment is a collective effort, and your commitment to continuous learning will contribute to positive change. As you remain receptive to new ideas and insights, you'll enrich your perspectives and actively contribute to building a more diverse and equitable work environment for everyone.

Industry Insight

Ashley Ridgeway-Washington,
Title, Company

Demonstrating a commitment to DEI through your resume is both art and science. Here are a few ways to ensure your resume conveys inclusivity as an integral component of your employee brand.

Describe your leadership experiences using language that is inclusive by design. If you find conveying your commitment to DEI through your resume challenging, focus on inclusive language to describe leadership competencies, transferrable skills, and command of soft skills.

Avoid dishonesty at all costs. *Experienced recruiters will be able to detect embellishments. Concerns about honesty could undermine your overall credibility.*

Dive deep and double-check. *Identify work that may indirectly support DEI and make the correlation as you describe the work. Spend time thinking about projects that require cross-functional collaboration, working across geographies, or accessing diverse customers. You may have advanced DEI in the workplace in more ways than you thought.*

Quantify your accomplishments and describe your role in the outcome. *When describing experiences, quantify your achievements and detail your contributions. If you led a planning committee that delivered a mentoring program that contributed to increased promotion rates among Gen. Z employees, say that with specificity. For example, 'I led the reverse mentoring selection committee. This program delivered an integral component of our generational diversity strategy. Our efforts resulted in a 7% increase in Gen Z. promotions and helped increase* *retention among Gen. Z by 22%. I am so proud of our accomplishments.'*

By following these tips, you can show hiring managers that you're committed to diversity, equity, and inclusion as a way of working. This will make you a more attractive candidate for companies that prioritize DEI.

Adapted Excerpt from RESTAGED

I am a firm believer that it is the choices we make or fail to make that change our circumstances. Seemingly small changes can make a tremendous difference. However, even the smallest changes can require significant effort. In my experience, small amounts of effort sustained over a period have been the best approach to achieve lasting results. I attended Florida A&M University's School of Business & Industry where our motto was "No excuse is acceptable. No amount of effort is adequate until proven effective." To this day, I keep that motto top of mind. In my opinion, this should be the motto for DEI. For far too long, we have accepted excuses in place of effort.

One of the reasons you may have a perceived or actual weakness related to DEI is because you have blind spots. Blinds spots can be hard to find because they are often buried in denial. The sometimes-unpleasant nature of the truth and perception that feedback is accusatory creates an inability to recognize or unwillingness to deal with the proverbial elephant in the room. Denial is a close relative of fear, which functions to protect our self-image and requires a substantial investment of energy. Redirecting that energy to search for your blind spots can be difficult, but it can lead to significant insights. However, identifying your own blind spots is an exercise in contradiction. If you can see them, they are no longer blind to you.

So how do you find your blind spots? Blind spots are repetitive experiences that make you question why something always seems to happen to you. For example: you always have a terrible boss, you always end up working on teams with people you don't get along with, or people consistently perceive you differently than you see yourself. If the evidence suggests you have blind spots, you can try to eliminate them by asking yourself, "Why am I afraid to see my role in these situations?" While tackling your fears often leads to meaningful insights, the better approach may be soliciting feedback from others as feedback helps illuminate blind spots. Not only does it help you build knowledge about yourself, it also informs you of what you don't know, which can be used to create a learning journey. The more diverse the individuals are who provide the feedback, the better you will be able to see where there is consistency and divergence. Even though honest feedback can be valuable, most of us must force ourselves to ask for it. Any form of feedback is scary, but the kind that tackles your blind spots can be unbearable. That's why, before you ask for honest feedback, you should have a strategy in place.

The best tool for handling solicited feedback is choice. You can choose the date, time, location, length, topics, and objectives. For the feedback session to be meaningful, be in a place where you are open to receiving it. Here are some other tips you can use while receiving feedback.

Quick Tips for Soliciting and Utilizing Feedback

- Consider the source and its intent.
- Listen actively to what is said and how it is said.
- Summarize what you hear to confirm you are interpreting it correctly.
- Ask clarifying questions.
- Focus on the facts and not opinions.
- Identify one or two things you agree with that you can act on and put a plan in place.

- Don't be defensive, understand the feedback is meant to help you identify your blind spots.

The range of what we think and do is limited by what we fail to notice. And because we fail to notice that we fail to notice, there is little we can do to change: until we notice how failing to notice shapes our thoughts and deeds. —R.D. Laing

Before we dive into the sample questions, here is a spoiler alert. You will not find any answers to the sample questions in this book. We went back and forth on this decision, but ultimately we wrote this book to encourage deep thought and reflection and not memorization of sample answers to by-pass the competencies we want the questions to shed light on. The answers to the questions should stem from your personal, lived, or learned experiences. If you are struggling to find answers, that means you've identified DEI blind spots in your leadership profile. While there is still much work to do around DEI on a global perspective, it will become increasingly more difficult to build a career in a world where the U.S. is a majority-minority nation, and 85% of the world's population is in Asia, Africa, and Latin America.

However, don't be disappointed, because what we are willing to share is what an organization may be looking for by asking you these questions and insights from industry professionals who are committed to advancing DEI. These questions are intended to help you **pick someone good at the job and not just good at the interview.**

PART III

CHAPTER VI

9 DEI Questions On Creating a Diverse and Inclusive Workforce

An interviewer may ask you about how you have created a diverse and inclusive workplace in your previous experience for several reasons:

Assessing your soft skills. Creating a diverse and inclusive workplace requires a certain set of skills, like empathy, open-mindedness, and the ability to understand and appreciate different perspectives.

One of the skills we'd like to emphasize is empathy. Empathetic leaders can understand and connect with their team members on a deeper level. By demonstrating empathy, leaders can foster trust, strengthen relationships, and create a supportive and collaborative work environment. When leaders show empathy, they demonstrate that they care about their employees' well-being and understand their challenges.

Empathy allows leaders to effectively communicate with their team members. By understanding others' perspectives and emotions, empathetic leaders can tailor their communication style, choose appropriate language, and deliver messages in a way that inspires and motivates their team members.

Empathetic leaders are also skilled at handling conflicts and problem-solving because they can see issues from different perspectives. By empathizing with all parties involved, leaders can find mutually beneficial solutions, promote open communication, and create a positive conflict resolution environment. During periods of change and uncertainty, empathetic leaders provide reassurance and stability, tending to the emotions and concerns of their team while remaining focused on achieving organizational goals. In cultivating these soft skills, leaders can create a truly inclusive and supportive workplace, empowering their teams to thrive and contribute to the overall success of the organization.

Culture fit. Organizations assess employees for culture fit to ensure that new hires align with the organization's values, norms, and working style. The idea behind culture fit suggests that individuals who share similar beliefs, attitudes, and behaviors with existing employees and the company's culture are more likely to excel and positively impact the organization's achievements. However, there has been an increasing discussion and evolving perspective regarding the potential drawbacks of exclusively assessing employees based on culture fit. Some concerns and criticisms include:

- **Lack of diversity and inclusion:** Placing too much emphasis on culture fit can inadvertently lead to homogeneous teams and limited diversity, which can stifle innovation and impede the inclusion of different perspectives.

- **Unconscious bias:** Assessing for culture fit may introduce unconscious biases in the hiring process, as evaluators might unconsciously favor candidates who resemble themselves or the existing workforce, leading to a lack of diversity and perpetuating existing inequalities. Overemphasis on fit can also lead to groupthink where everyone thinks and behaves similarly.

- **Inflexibility and resistance to change:** Prioritizing culture fit may discourage bringing in individuals with diverse experiences and alternative viewpoints, hindering organizational growth and adaptation to new challenges.

- **Exclusion of qualified candidates:** The most significant concern when using fit as an indicator is that applicants from diverse backgrounds may be excluded because they do not align with the organization's norms or values, especially if the organization is not progressive on dimensions of DEI. . Consequently, valuable talent that could contribute to the organization's growth and success may be overlooked and underutilized.

Recent evidence and research highlight the effectiveness of a more inclusive hiring approach that emphasizes cultural add over culture fit. By celebrating the unique perspectives candidates can bring to the organization, this approach proves to be more successful in building diverse and thriving teams. Rather than prioritizing conformity to the existing culture, the focus is on seeking candidates who can enrich the workplace with new perspectives, skills, and experiences that complement and enhance the overall organizational culture.

Problem-solving abilities. Creating a diverse and inclusive workplace can also involve addressing issues such as unconscious bias, discrimination, and harassment. By asking questions on this topic, the interviewer is trying to understand your problem-solving abilities and how you approached and resolved issues in the past.

Leadership potential. If you are applying for a leadership position, the interviewer may be interested in understanding your leadership style and how you have motivated and inspired teams and created a diverse and inclusive workplace.

Sample Questions

1. Can you describe a time when you identified a gap in diversity and inclusion within your workplace and took action to address it?

2. What strategies have you used in the past to promote diversity and inclusivity in your team or workplace?

3. Have you ever had to navigate a difficult conversation or conflict related to diversity and inclusion in the workplace? Can you share how you handled it?

4. Can you give an example of how you have actively sought out and welcomed diverse perspectives and opinions on a project or team?

5. How have you worked to ensure that all team members feel valued and included, regardless of their background or identity?

6. How has your personal or professional experience prepared you to advance our commitment to diversity and inclusion?

7. Can you describe a time when you worked with a team member who had a different background or perspective from you, and how you leveraged those differences to improve a project or outcome?

8. How have you addressed unconscious bias or microaggressions in the workplace, either as a leader or as part of a team?

9. In your opinion, what are some of the most effective ways to foster a culture of diversity and inclusivity in the workplace, and how have you contributed to those efforts in the past?

Industry Insight

Benson Fayehun, Executive Director, Merck

As a passionate advocate for diversity, equity, and inclusion, I've witnessed the incredible impact from leaders embracing diversity and creating an inclusive workplace. Not only is it the right thing to do, but it also brings tangible benefits to the business. Inclusive leaders understand that diversity fuels innovation. They create an environment where every individual feels valued, fostering a rich tapestry of perspectives that drives creativity and opens new opportunities.

Inclusive leadership is like a dance—a joyful celebration of diversity. It involves championing equality and infusing every step with empathy, respect, and openness. By creating an environment that embraces diversity, inclusive leaders unlock the full potential of their teams.

Inclusive leaders walk the talk. They take concrete actions to champion diversity and equity. They implement policies that promote inclusivity and provide equal opportunities for all. They break down barriers, challenge biases, and create spaces for underrepresented voices to shine. By aligning their words with meaningful actions, they create a culture where diversity is not just a buzzword but a guiding principle.

Active listening is a superpower of inclusive leaders. They seek diverse perspectives, challenge assumptions, and tap into the collective wisdom of their team. By learning from others and leveraging this wealth of knowledge, they create a harmonious and innovative culture. They inspire others to bring their true selves to work, fostering an inclusive culture where diversity is celebrated.

CHAPTER VII

9 DEI Questions On Developing Cultural Competency

The origin of cultural competency can be traced back to the field of cross-cultural psychology and the work of anthropologists, sociologists, and psychologists who studied the impact of culture on human behavior. It emerged as a concept in the 1980s and 1990s when professionals realized the importance of understanding and respecting cultural differences in various domains, including healthcare, education, and business.

Cultural competency refers to the ability to understand, appreciate, and effectively work with people from different cultures. It involves being aware of one's own cultural biases, attitudes, and beliefs, and actively working to develop the knowledge and skills necessary to navigate diverse cultural contexts. An interviewer may ask about how you developed your cultural competency to understand your learning process and commitment, as well as how well you might work with colleagues, clients, and customers from diverse backgrounds. They may also want to understand how you would adapt your communication and behavior to work effectively with people from different cultures. Your responses will demonstrate your openness to learning about different cultures, your ability to adapt to different communication styles, and your understanding of the importance of cultural competence in the workplace.

Industry Insight

Candace Cooper-Williams, Executive Coach and Culture Champion, Can Will Consulting

Developing cultural competency requires an ongoing commitment to learning, applying, and adapting your leadership style to various cultural elements, including their intersection. The interview process is an excellent opportunity to communicate the importance of cultural competence as a leadership enabler and assess if candidates have the hard and soft skills needed to lead an organization serving an increasingly diverse customer base.

Advancing diversity, equity, and inclusion requires leaders with vision, empathy, and integrity to shift the cultural versus simply "tick the box" on activities that don't lead to sustainable change. Embedding in-depth, nuanced questions on DEI will allow you identify the candidate that can usher in long-term success in an increasingly diverse and dynamic world.

Sample Questions

1. Can you describe a time when you had to work with individuals from a different culture than your own? What did you do to ensure effective communication and collaboration?

2. How do you educate yourself on cultural differences and practices? Do you have any examples of how this knowledge has helped you in your work or personal life?

3. Can you describe a situation where you misunderstood or misinterpreted someone from a different culture than your own? How did you address this situation and what did you learn from it?

4. How do you adapt your style to effectively communicate with individuals from different cultures? Can you provide an example of a time when you had to adapt your communication style?

5. Can you describe a time when you had to navigate a difficult cross-cultural situation? How did you handle it and what did you learn from the experience?

6. How do you ensure that you do not impose your cultural beliefs or biases onto others? Can you provide an example of how you have avoided doing this in the past?

7. Can you describe a situation where you had to show empathy towards someone from a different cultural background than your own? How did you approach this situation?

8. How do you seek out and value diverse perspectives in your personal and professional life? Can you provide an example of how you have done this?

9. What steps do you take to continue learning and growing in your cultural competency? Can you provide an example of how you have implemented these steps in the past?

Industry Insight

Amy Gómez, Ph.D., SVP, Diversity Strategy, Klick Health

The importance of asking people-leader candidates about developing cultural competence cannot be overemphasized—it's a critical skill because of the significant benefits it generates both internally within the company culture and externally for the company's customers and shareholders.

Culturally competent people-leaders with responsibility for a single market establish and value a diverse team (across the multiple elements of diversity), operate with cultural humility, communicate effectively across cultural differences, and foster an environment of inclusion. People leaders with global responsibility across multiple markets understand and skillfully navigate the key cultural differences between their markets and foster more effective cross-country partnerships.

In both cases, the result is a culturally intelligent team well equipped to innovate product and services offerings that strategically cater to the needs of a diverse customer base. In short, culture competence is a key driver of innovation, which leads to stronger growth. Identifying leaders who understand the importance of cultural competence, who possess it and prioritize its development within their teams supports long-term sustainable company success.

CHAPTER VIII

9 DEI Questions on Leading Diverse Teams

Diverse teams are critical in creating a dynamic and innovative workplace culture. Companies recognize that having a diverse team can bring different perspectives, ideas, and approaches to problem-solving, which can lead to more creative solutions and better outcomes. Leading a diverse team requires certain skills such as active listening, effective communication, intellectual curiosity, adaptability, empathy, and cultural sensitivity. An interviewer may want to assess whether you possess these skills and have experience working with people from different cultural, ethnic, and social backgrounds.

Inclusion is an important aspect of diversity, and the interviewer may be interested in knowing how you ensure that all team members feel valued, respected, and included. They may want to learn about the strategies you use to ensure that everyone's voice is heard and that everyone has an equal opportunity to contribute. A good leader can adapt their style to the unique perspectives and experiences that each team member brings to the table.

Industry Insight

Sonia Thompson, CEO, Thompson Media Group.
Chief Consultant, Sonia Thompson, Inc.

It's nice to see more companies focusing on building representative teams, as it is fast becoming a business imperative. However, just because you have a diverse team doesn't mean you'll automatically reap the benefits of one.

You must know how to lead a team of diverse talent in a way that enables everyone on the team to thrive, where everyone knows their voice, unique experiences, and points of view are welcomed and needed. And you must know how to cultivate a psychologically safe culture where people know they don't have to code switch, hide parts of themselves, or question whether they can say something that challenges accepted operating norms.

Diverse teams thrive consistently only when leaders cultivate and nurture them to do so. This is a skill leaders need to verify during the interview process, by having candidates showcase examples of demonstrated proficiency in these areas.

Sample Questions

1. How do you ensure that all team members feel valued and respected, regardless of their background?

2. Can you provide an example of a time when you successfully led a diverse team to achieve a common goal?

3. How do you encourage open communication and collaboration within a diverse team?

4. What steps do you take to address any conflicts or misunderstandings that may arise among team members from different cultural backgrounds?

5. How do you adapt your leadership style to accommodate different communication styles and cultural norms within your team?

6. Can you discuss a time when you had to address bias or discrimination within your team, and how you handled it?

7. How do you ensure that diversity and inclusion are incorporated into the hiring and promotion processes for your team?

8. Can you discuss a time when you had to balance the needs and perspectives of multiple diverse stakeholders on a project or initiative?

9. How do you encourage team members to share their unique perspectives and ideas, even if they differ from your own?

9 DEI Questions on Psychological Safety

The COVID-19 pandemic triggered what is now called the Great Resignation and may have also contributed to the rise of "quiet-quitting."
When individuals who resigned during the pandemic were questioned about their reasons for leaving, many felt excluded, undervalued, disrespected, untrusted, or uncared for as key factors influencing their decisions. The majority who felt this way happened to be women and those from underrepresented ethnic groups. As we discussed in earlier chapters, gender and ethnically diverse teams contribute to significantly better financial performance, product innovation, and employee retention. Diverse teams also help organizations anticipate, manage, and adjust to risk in times of uncertainty. In fact, organizations with gender-diverse

boards outperformed those who were not during the peak of COVID-19-related negative market sentiment.

You may be asking what this has to do with psychological safety. While diverse teams can generate more ideas and perspectives to improve decision-making, this only happens when those perspectives are welcomed, heard, and valued.

Why are organizations asking?

An interviewer might ask about your ability to create psychological safety because it is an important skill in building and maintaining a positive and productive work environment. Psychological safety refers to the feeling of trust, mutual respect, and confidence that individuals have within a team or organization, where they feel it OK to take risks, admit mistakes, and speak up and share ideas and concerns without fear of negative consequences.

Creating psychological safety is particularly important in collaborative work settings where team members need to work together effectively, share ideas openly, and feel supported by their colleagues. Employers recognize that creating a culture of psychological safety can improve team performance, increase innovation and creativity, and reduce turnover and absenteeism.

Therefore, an interviewer might ask about your ability to create psychological safety to assess your communication and leadership skills, your ability to build relationships and trust with others, your approach to conflict resolution and problem-solving, and your ability demonstrate humility and empathy. Your responses will reveal whether there are blind spots that could undermine your ability to successfully participate on or lead a team.

It is important to call out that psychological safety is more art than science. It is often co-created by the team or triggered by an unexpected circumstance the team must face together. Given the strong link between DEI, psychological safety, and good management practices, it is important to ask these questions.

Two watchouts worth mentioning are that a psychologically safe environment isn't necessarily a polite or nice. In these types of organizations, a lot often goes unsaid because candor is not invited or rewarded. Additionally, feeling a sense of belonging doesn't mean there won't be moments of discomfort. If it often these moments where the most learning happens. Psychological safety, just like DEI, requires vulnerability and health relationship with risk.

Sample Questions

1. What is your understanding of psychological safety, and how important do you think it is for teams to have this type of environment?

2. Can you describe a time when you felt psychologically unsafe in a work setting? How did you handle the situation, and what could have been done to create a more supportive environment?

3. How do you typically encourage team members to share their opinions and ideas, especially if they may be different from the rest of the team?

4. What steps do you take to build trust and establish open communication with team members?

5. How do you address conflict within a team, and what strategies do you use to ensure that all voices are heard and respected?

6. What are some warning signs that a team may be lacking in psychological safety, and how do you address these issues?

7. How do you ensure that team members feel comfortable bringing up mistakes or failures without fear of negative repercussions?

8. Can you discuss a time when you had to give difficult feedback to a team member? How did you approach the conversation, and what steps did you take to ensure that the team member felt supported?

9. How do you encourage team members to take risks and try new approaches, even if they may not be successful? How do you provide support and encouragement when things don't go as planned?

Industry Insight

Damien Carter, GSK, DEI Champion

The Covid-19 Pandemic, market fluctuations, and geopolitical environment has made resilience a required skill for organizations and leaders. In today's business climate, the only certainty is uncertainty. To survive uncertainty, organizations need a culture where it is safe to speak up to share ideas, differing perspectives, or raise concerns related to ethics and compliance. This type of culture is often described as being psychologically safe.

A leader who excels at creating a psychologically safe culture does so by demonstrating high levels of integrity and being radically inclusive. I like to use questions to address ethical dilemmas such as what happens if we do or don't do something. This creates a safe space to evaluate both sides of a decision. Examples of radical inclusion includes calling out bias, equitably providing resources and support, and respecting and valuing people for their differences.

Psychological safety requires intentionality as our instinctive human response is to exercise caution in unfamiliar environments until we know it is safe. This caution causes people to operate from a place of fear which leads to mistrust, the perfect combination for a toxic work environment. Inclusion counters fear by letting people know that not only is it safe, but they are welcomed. Like trust, psychological safety takes time to build and even longer to rebuild. The best way to build trust is by being consistent in your words and actions and extending trust before requiring it.

CHAPTER X

DEI Questions to Ask the Interviewer

W hy should candidates ask DEI questions? After successfully answering all the questions posed by interviewers, which hopefully included several of the DEI questions we've shared, candidates should take the opportunity to ask interviewers questions regarding diversity and inclusion.

Asking DEI questions during the interview can benefit you in several ways:

- **Shows your interest.** Asking DEI questions during the interview conveys its importance to you and presents an opportunity to assess how important it is to the hiring manager and the company. As these questions are infrequently asked to interviewers, doing so could leave a positive impression on the interviewer and cause you to stand out from other candidates.

- **Clarifies doubts.** You may have done some research but still have doubts about the leader, department, or organization that you would like to clarify. By asking DEI questions, you can get a better understanding of the job expectations, the leader's management style, company culture, and opportunities for growth.

- **Provides insights.** Asking insightful DEI questions can also provide you with valuable information about headwinds and tailwinds in the organization.

- **Shows your research.** Asking DEI questions that demonstrate you have thoroughly researched the organization, leader, and role will communicate your commitment to the organization and also your values.

Overall, asking DEI questions empowers candidates to make informed decisions about potential employers, ensuring they find a workplace that celebrates diversity and fosters an inclusive and equitable environment.

Sample Questions

1. How does the organization approach diversity, equity, and inclusion, and what steps have been taken to foster an inclusive workplace culture?

2. How does the organization measure the success of its diversity, equity, and inclusion initiatives, and what specific goals has it set?

3. What kind of training or support does the organization provide to help employees understand and embrace diversity and inclusion?

4. How does the organization respond to incidents of discrimination, harassment, or bias, and what kind of policies are in place to prevent them?

5. How diverse is the leadership team, and what steps is the organization taking to promote diversity in leadership roles?

6. How does the organization ensure that job postings and hiring practices are inclusive and avoid implicit bias?

7. How does the organization seek diverse perspectives and input when making decisions and shaping the culture?

8. Are there any employee-led diversity and inclusion initiatives or affinity groups within the organization, and how are they supported?

9. How does the organization ensure that all employees, regardless of their background or identity, have equal opportunities for growth and advancement?

Industry Insight

Brandon J. Handy, Vice President, Talent Management, BBB Industries, LLC

In my experience as both an HR professional and as a job candidate, the only way to truly understand the workplace culture is to ask very direct questions, seeking both understanding and examples of what to expect. What a job candidate is really digging into is belongingness. Once they are there at the office, on the production floor, or working remotely, what are the systems in place that will help them belong to the team and the company as a whole?

Do the leaders of the company both at the line level as well as senior executives make this an important part of their daily operating model? Published reports and white papers on a company's DEI efforts can only tell part of the story. The discussion during the interview process can help fill in the remaining blanks.

CHAPTER XI

Removing Bias from the Interview Process

Removing bias from the interview process is critical to advancing diversity, equity, and inclusion in the workplace. A fair and unbiased interview process ensures that all candidates are evaluated on the same criteria and that they have an equal opportunity to demonstrate their skills and qualifications. When bias is present in the process, qualified applicants from underrepresented groups may be misunderstood and therefore overlooked, leading to a less diverse and inclusive workforce. To mitigate these risks, organizations should implement strategies to minimize and altogether eliminate bias at every stage in the interview process.

Below are several of the risks associated with bias in the interview process.

- **Legal.** If bias is present in the process, it can lead to allegations of discrimination and legal action against the organization. This can damage the company's reputation and lead to significant financial and legal consequences.

- **Employee Morale.** When bias is present in the interview process, it can lead to a perception of unfairness among candidates who are not selected for the job. This can also impact the morale of current employees, particularly those from underrepresented groups, who may feel undervalued and excluded.

- **Retention and Revenue.** When bias is present in the interview process, it can lead to poor decision-making and hiring the wrong candidate for the job. This may result in decreased productivity, increased turnover, and lost revenue.

As research into the role bias plays in the hiring process has increased, we now have evidence-based suggestions companies can take to remove it.

- **Develop a Structured Interview Process.** A standardized interview process that includes a set of predetermined questions asked of all prospective hires helps ensure candidates are evaluated on the same criteria and reduces the risk of bias. Research shows that structured interviews are twice as effective as unstructured interviews in predicting job performance.

- **Blind Screening.** Blind screening involves removing any identifying information from resumes, such as name, gender identity, age, race, sexual orientation, disability status, or even educational institution. This helps eliminate any unconscious biases that may arise based on these factors. A study by the National Bureau of Economic Research found that removing identifying information from resumes, such as name and address, significantly increased the probability of minority candidates being selected for interviews.

- **Use Objective Criteria.** Developing clear and objective criteria for evaluating candidates, such as specific skills, experience, and qualifications required for the job helps reduce the risk of subjective biases in the interview process. A study by Harvard Business Review found that when recruiters focused on specific job-related criteria, such as work experience, they were less likely to be influenced by irrelevant information, such as a candidate's hobbies.

- **Use Diverse Interview Panels.** Diverse interview panels with members from different backgrounds and experiences can help reduce bias in the hiring process and can also bring different perspectives to the process. A study by the National Bureau of Economic Research found that when there was a diverse panel, the probability of hiring a minority candidate increased by 50%.

- **Conduct Behavioral Interviews.** Behavioral interviews are designed to assess how candidates have responded to past situations and how they would respond to similar situations in the future. This approach helps evaluate candidates on their actions rather than on assumptions based on demographic characteristics. A study by the Society for Industrial and Organizational Psychology found that behavioral interviews have a validity coefficient of 0.55, compared to 0.38 for unstructured interviews.

- **Use Validated Assessment Tools.** A study by the American Psychological Association found that using validated assessment tools, such as cognitive and personality tests, can help reduce bias in the hiring process. Administering objective assessments of candidates' abilities removes subjective judgment and allows employers to evaluate applicants on objective criteria.

- **Provide Unconscious Bias Training.** A study by the Journal of Applied Psychology found that providing unconscious bias training to recruiters and hiring managers can increase their awareness of potential biases and help them make more objective decisions.

- **Monitor and Track Diversity Metrics.** A study by the Harvard Business Review found that companies that tracked diversity metrics were more likely to have a diverse workforce. This approach should be applied to the hiring process, tracking metrics related to gender identity and ethnicity as an example, to help identify potential areas of bias.

- **Be Transparent About the Process.** A study by Glassdoor found that job candidates were more likely to trust the hiring process when it was transparent and consistent.

- **Audit the Interview Process.** It is important to evaluate the interview process regularly to identify any potential areas of bias and adjust as needed. A study by the Society for Human Resource Management found that regular evaluation of the hiring process can help ensure the process remains fair and objective.

As mentioned in Part II, the answers to the proposed DEI interview questions were not provided. Therefore, how will one know if the answer the candidate provided is in fact a good one? As the interviewer, you shouldn't look for good answers, but instead an honest answer that should be personal and supported by evidence. The same way a candidate can speak at length, from memory, and with pride about their accomplishments related to projects and awards, if they have been committed to advancing DEI, they should be able to do the same. Having diverse candidate slates, diverse interviewer panels, and incorporating DEI questions into a structured behavioral interview will produce insights that will improve and simplify the selection process.

In Closing

Before we commenced the journey of writing the book you are close to finishing, we really questioned whether the world needed another book on DEI. Each year, between 500,000 to 1 million books are published through traditional publishers. If you include self-published titles, the number grows to about 4 million. Despite knowing the odds of our book becoming a best-seller were slim, we proceeded anyway. We decided to write it first and foremost for ourselves. The writing process allowed us to increase our knowledge and challenged us to find a way to communicate that knowledge to all of you. Throughout the process, we also developed empathy for each other's lived, intersectional, experience.

During one of our many conversations, we discussed our definition of success for the book. We didn't land on copies sold or some dollar figure. It was something more powerful, and possibly more achievable—changing one person's beliefs and behavior.

> *Books are a form of political action. Books are knowledge. Books are reflection. Books change your mind.* —Toni Morrison

While we defined several DEI terms upfront, we didn't want this book to be about labels. We wanted change. Borrowing from the Fogg Behavioral Model (B=MAP), we focused on outlining several reasons that should motivate someone to change, linked it with something that is relatively easy to do (ask someone a question), and identified two prompts (you need to hire someone, and we have given you the questions). The combination of these factors should make it easy for everyone to change.

If you missed this, here is a quick recap. Your motivation to embrace DEI can be anchored to profit or loss, hope or fear, acceptance or rejection. We chose the interview process because we wanted to remove any excuse about DEI being difficult to implement. Every day, interviews are conducted all over the world. They do not require physical effort, they are not taxing to the brain, they do not require a significant investment of time or money, they are a universally accepted organizational norm, and most have either been interviewed or interviewed someone else. Finally, when we post a job, we are immediately triggered to know we will need to interview someone and that we will need questions to have an equitable process.

While we acknowledge that this may seem too simple to be effective, consider the fact that the job interview dates to ancient times. The concept of assessing potential candidates for positions can be traced back to ancient civilizations. For example, in ancient China and Greece, prospective government officials had to go through interviews to demonstrate their knowledge and qualifications for public service. During the industrial revolution, as companies expanded and sought to hire workers for various roles, they needed a more systematic way to evaluate candidates. In the early twentieth century, the concept of behavioral interviewing began to emerge. Psychologist Hugo Münsterberg suggested using interviews to assess candidates' personality and behavioral traits to predict job performance. In the mid-twentieth century, with the advent of antidiscrimination laws, interviews faced scrutiny for potential bias and discrimination. Efforts were made to standardize the interview process to reduce bias.

Over time, various interview techniques and

formats have been developed, including structured interviews, situational interviews, and behavioral interviews. Today, job interviews are a common and essential part of the hiring process across various industries and job sectors.

While the job interview has a long history, it continues to evolve as organizations seek to refine their hiring practices and ensure they select the best candidates for their teams. Additionally, advancements in technology have led to the emergence of artificial intelligence-based interview tools, and more data-driven approaches to candidate assessment, which if left unchecked, can replicate human bias.

So, the interview is here to stay, and if we hardwire these questions into the system, so is DEI.

A lot of thought went into our approach because we are aware of the growing notion of DEI fatigue. DEI fatigue refers to the weariness, exhaustion, or resistance experienced by individuals or organizations when dealing with issues related to diversity, equity, and inclusion. It can manifest in various ways, such as employees feeling overwhelmed by continuous DEI discussions or initiatives, resistance to change, decreased engagement with DEI efforts, or even burnout from the emotional labor involved in addressing these sensitive topics. Causes of DEI fatigue can vary but often include:

1. **Overload of DEI Initiatives.** When organizations introduce too many DEI initiatives without proper planning or resources, it can lead to fatigue. Employees may perceive these efforts as performative or superficial if they don't see meaningful results.

2. **Emotional Toll.** Conversations about DEI can be emotionally draining, particularly for those who are directly affected by the issues being discussed or have experienced discrimination themselves.

3. **Tokenism.** Feeling like a diversity hire or being tokenized can create feelings of isolation and burnout for employees from underrepresented backgrounds.

4. **Resistance to Change.** Some employees might resist DEI efforts due to discomfort or fear of losing privilege or power in the workplace.

5. **Lack of Support.** If employees perceive that DEI efforts lack support from leadership or are not given enough priority, they may become disheartened and fatigued.

6. **Unrealistic Expectations.** Setting unrealistic

expectations or timelines for achieving DEI goals can create frustration and burnout.

7. **Lack of progression.** When DEI efforts do not lead to tangible changes in the workplace, it may cause disillusionment and frustration with the lack of positive movement.

We have personally experienced and witnessed the detrimental impact of DEI fatigue on an organization's DEI efforts through decreased engagement of employees from all groups. The lack of progress and unfounded excuses for it saps motivation. This often leads to increased turnover, especially for leaders from diverse communities, which casts a long shadow over the organization, impacting the workplace culture.

The approaches we are proposing can help make organizations immune to DEI fatigue because these questions are part of the moral fiber of organizations. It's in their DNA. These are not DEI questions at the end of the day, they are values-based questions. Moreover, when organizations create a culture of shared responsibility for DEI, it promotes sustainable progress and moves the needle forward.

Imagine if we changed DEI to values. This is how a values-based approach could combat DEI fatigue:

1. **Leadership Commitment:** Leadership must demonstrate a genuine and sustained commitment to the **organizational values**. This involves providing necessary resources, setting realistic goals, and holding people accountable for progress.

2. **Clear Communication:** Transparent and open communication about the **organization's values** can help address concerns, manage expectations, and reinforce the importance of the initiatives.

3. **Training and Education:** Providing ongoing training and education on the **organization's values** can help create a more inclusive and understanding work environment. This includes unconscious bias training, cultural competence workshops, and inclusive leadership development.

4. **Employee Support:** Offer support systems, such as Employee Assistance Programs (EAPs), where employees can seek help for emotional and mental well-being.

5. **Employee Involvement:** Encourage employees to actively participate in shaping initiatives to strengthen adoption of **organizational values.** Their involvement in decision-making can increase their sense of ownership and engagement.

6. **Celebrate Successes:** Acknowledge and celebrate progress and successes in **organizational values** both big and small, to keep motivation and momentum high.

7. **Pace and Balance:** Avoid overwhelming employees with too many organizational values initiatives simultaneously. Focus on a few key values and allow employees time to process and adapt.

A values-based approach can eliminate DEI fatigue by infusing a sense of purpose and meaning into diversity, equity, and inclusion initiatives. When organizations prioritize DEI as a fundamental value and align it with their core principles, it becomes a collective responsibility embraced by everyone, from leadership to employees at all levels. This shift in mindset creates a culture where DEI is not perceived as an isolated initiative but as an integral part of the organization's identity and mission.

Moreover, a values-based approach to DEI promotes transparency and accountability. Organizations prioritizing DEI as a core value are more likely to hold themselves accountable for progress, measure results, and share their efforts with stakeholders. This transparency helps build trust and credibility, reducing skepticism and fatigue that may arise when progress is not adequately communicated.

As we reach the conclusion of this book, our genuine hope is that the insights, strategies, and experiences woven throughout these chapters will ignite a deep sense of inspiration and empowerment within you. We encourage you to embrace the role of a proactive advocate for diversity, equity, and inclusion in your workplaces. By championing DEI principles and values, you can cultivate environments where everyone feels welcomed, valued, and supported, leading to remarkable personal and organizational growth and success. Together, let us embark on this transformative journey to construct an equitable and inclusive future for all.

Amateurs practice until they get it right. Professionals practice until they can't get it wrong —unknown

Printed in the USA
CPSIA information can be obtained
at www.ICGtesting.com
LVHW040514171023
761213LV00004B/125

9 781957 092836